Oxford Medicine:
A Walk Through Nine
Centuries

Eric Sidebottom

April 2015

Dr Eric Sidebottom

Map of Walk Sites

1. Magdalen College
2. Botanic (Physic) Garden
3. Penicillin Rose Garden
4. Examination Schools
5. Morris Garage
6. New College (of St Mary)
7. Holywell Cemetery
8. Queen's College
9. University College
10. High Street
11. Merton College
12. Beam Hall and Thomas Willis
13. Christ Church
14. Oriel College
15. Brasenose College
16. St Mary's Church and Catte Street
17. All Souls College
18. Radcliffe Camera (Library)
19. Bodleian Library (Duke Humfrey)
20. Sheldonian Theatre
21. Old Ashmolean Museum
22. Balliol College
23. New Bodleian Library
24. Wadham College
25. University Museum of Natural History
26. The Radcliffe Science Library
27. Rhodes House
28. Dorothy Hodgkin Plaque
29. Physiology
30. Biochemistry
31. Pathology

 Regular walk sites   *Diversion sites*

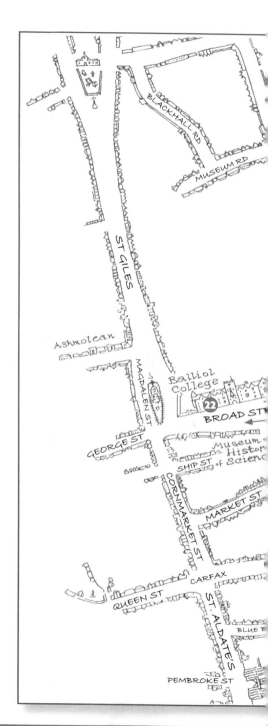

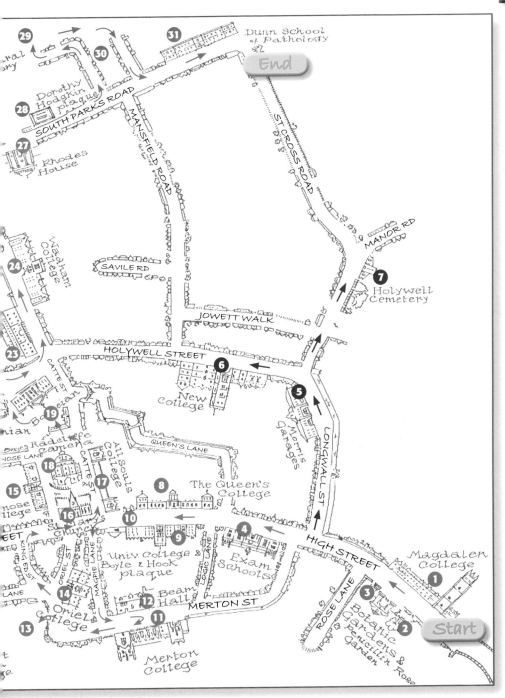

A catalogue record for this book is available from The British Library

ISBN 978-1-904202-05-9

Designed and set by Oxford Art and Design, Oxford
Photographs by the author (unless otherwise stated)
Printed and bound in Great Britain by Information Press, Eynsham, Oxford

Acknowledgements

Many people have contributed to the conception, gestation, and delivery of this small book. First, I must thank Jayne Todd, who cajoled me into turning the notes for the original walk into a manuscript. Various members of the Oxford Alumni Council added suggestions. Claire Greszczuk drew the delightful map of central Oxford illustrating the recommended route of the walk. Robin Roberts-Gant and Louise Allison introduced me to the ideas and execution of design, and Jackie Gray guided me through the publication process. My wife, Margaret, has patiently listened to my grumbles about low-resolution photographs, copyright issues, and various other irritations that befall inexperienced authors.

For permission to publish photographs, I am grateful to: The Master and Fellows of Balliol College, Oxford; The Dean and Students of Christ Church, Oxford; The President and Fellows of Magdalen College, Oxford; The Warden and Fellows of Merton College, Oxford; The Principal and Fellows of Somerville College, Oxford; The Ashmolean Museum, University of Oxford; Oxfordshire County Council; Sue Chaundy; The Oxford Mail & Times.

If I am notified that I have unwittingly infringed any copyrights, I should be pleased to amend the acknowledgments in any future edition.

I am most grateful to Microscope Services Ltd for generous sponsorship.

Contents

Nobel Prize-winners   ● *Diversion sites*

*Nobel Prize-winners   ● Diversion sites

The Bridge of Sighs

A request, made some years ago by the Oxford University Medical School office, that I give a guided walk illustrating Oxford's medical history to a group of American physicians and their spouses, set me thinking what a wonderfully scenic, and intellectually stimulating place the centre of Oxford is. The first walk was duly planned and executed and, as a result, several more were commissioned. But now, in addition, I have been challenged by colleagues to describe that walk in words and pictures. Here is the result.

It can perhaps best be described as one man's rather eclectic collection of the fascinating places and people associated with Oxford's medical past. The selection of which individuals and colleges to include may be considered somewhat arbitrary; for example the decision to leave out the two colleges with which I have been most involved, Corpus and Lincoln, was a difficult one. However, I believe that what is almost undeniable is that to wander through the centre of Oxford (preferably on a fine day), and to consider its history, especially its medical history, is an uplifting experience. I should perhaps confess to having exercised a certain amount of architectural license, in that the medical associations of some of the buildings are rather tenuous, but it did seem invidious not to mention some of the more beautiful ones as we stroll from one medically-associated site to the next.

Naturally, I hope that some of the readers of this little book will be sufficiently stimulated to try the walk for themselves, and that they might derive at least some of the pleasure that I have done from this light exercise.

The walk can obviously be started anywhere en route and tailored according to time and tastes. The suggested start, however, outside the Botanic Garden gazing up at Magdalen Tower, has the advantage not only of being a beautiful meeting place, but also of immediately introducing the nine centuries span of the walk, from the 12th century hospital ruins under Magdalen Tower, via the 17th century Botanic Garden to the 20th century Penicillin Memorial Garden.

The 'Sites', numbered from 1 to 31 are within easy reach on my recommended 2 hour stroll but some of the 'Outlier Sites', lettered A to L, are outside this range and visits to them will require additional time and planning.

An added benefit of a project such as this, is that one inevitably meets lots of interesting people who have suggestions about new historical figures or sites that might be appropriate to mention on the walk. To these people, some of them even anonymous to me, and to my many professional colleagues from whom I have sought advice, I give my grateful thanks. Any mistakes or deficiencies are entirely my own responsibility but I should be grateful for suggestions about how I might improve this little book.

There is a wealth of literature on Oxford's buildings and its alumni and a great deal of information now available on the web. For my purpose, the most useful source about people was *The Book of Oxford*, a small handbook printed specially for the 1936 meeting of the BMA in Oxford,

Botanic Garden looking towards Magdalen College Tower

much of it written by R. T. Gunther. I also took occasional dips into Gunther's comprehensive, multi-volume *History of Science in Oxford*. For buildings, the *Clarendon Guide to Oxford* and the Royal Commission on Historical Monuments survey of the city of Oxford, served admirably. In addition, of course, I frequently consulted web sites of the University, its colleges, and the Oxford hospitals.

Eric Sidebottom

The recommended start of the walk is outside the Botanic Garden gazing across at Magdalen Tower.

The College was founded originally as Magdalen Hall half-way up the High Street in 1448, and moved to its present site in 1458.

The founder, William of Waynflete, was Bishop of Winchester and had already had a hand in the foundation of schools (he had been Provost of Eton) in which new educational ideas of the Renaissance era, as well as new methods of teaching, were tried out. For example, he introduced the teaching of Latin in the English language, and later pioneered the teaching of Greek. Waynflete was greatly influenced by Renaissance ideas about education, and as his ambitions grew, he managed to acquire a large tract of land beyond the walls of Oxford on which to build an entirely new College, dedicated to St Mary Magdalen.

He obtained permission from Henry VI to take over the buildings and lands of an ancient and decaying Hospital, dedicated to St. John the Baptist. The hospital was first mentioned in 1180 and refounded by Henry III in 1231 with a grant for a garden for the Jews outside the gates. Here the Founder established Magdalen College and

Magdalen College seen from the High Street

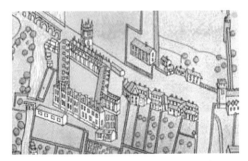

Richard Agas's Map of 1578 shows the lay-out of the medieval College, situated outside the city walls. The East Gate and the Walls appear in the right of the picture. From The Story of Magdalen *by Rena Gardiner (Copyright: Magdalen College, Oxford 2003)*

Notable Graduates and Fellows of Magdalen College

Joseph Addison *essayist*

Sir John Burdon Sanderson *first Professor of Physiology*

Charles Daubeny *doctor, chemist, botanist, geologist*

Lord Alfred Denning *judge*

Lord Alfred 'Bosie' Douglas *poet*

Sir John Eccles *1963 Nobel Prize in Medicine*

Lord Florey *1945 Nobel Prize in Medicine*

Edward Gibbon *historian*

Seamus Heaney *1995 Nobel Prize in Literature*

C.S. Lewis *writer*

Peter Medawar *1960 Nobel Prize in Medicine*

Dudley Moore *comedian*

Robert Robinson *1947 Nobel Prize in Chemistry*

Erwin Schrodinger *1933 Nobel Prize in Physics*

Charles Sherrington *1932 Nobel Prize in Medicine*

Hugh Sinclair *nutritionist*

Henry Tizard *chemist & President of College 1942-46*

Oscar Wilde *writer*

its associated Hall and School. Centuries later, the original Hall become incorporated into Hertford College but Magdalen College School flourishes to this day two hundred yards from its original site. Both the School and the College adopted and retain the arms of Waynflete as their own.

Magdalen was among the first colleges in Oxford to teach Science. Bishop Waynflete was profoundly interested in science – more than the founders of other colleges of the Renaissance era. It was the presence of many early physicians at Magdalen which led to the establishment in 1621 of the Physic Garden on Magdalen College land. Today it is the Oxford Botanic Garden (see Site 2 overleaf).

Two of the more worthy/interesting characters to inhabit Magdalen must have been:

Charles Daubeny

Daubeny was surely the quintessential Magdalen man. He arrived from Winchester in 1810 and died in Magdalen in 1867. Although he qualified in medicine and held a physician's post at the Radcliffe Infirmary, he was not an enthusiastic doctor and preferred the life of a scientist and teacher. At various times he held the Aldrichian chair of chemistry, the Sherardian chair of botany and the Sibthorpian chair of rural economy. He never achieved great scientific fame but nevertheless left a lasting legacy in that he was one of the dons who fought for, and eventually succeeded in establishing, an honours school of natural science and the building of the University Museum of Natural History, where all the sciences could have a base for teaching and research. In both these endeavours, of course, Henry Acland received more recognition. Daubeny is also remembered as the man responsible for planning and financing the building that bears his name (see Site 2 overleaf).

Hugh Sinclair, another quintessential Magdalen man, was elected as a Fellow in 1937, the year after he qualified in medicine; he remained attached to the college until his death in 1990. He must be regarded as one of Oxford's favourite 20th century eccentrics, probably principally remembered for his last great experiment, in which he set out to prove the virtues of the Inuit diet by eating seal meat regularly at Magdalen high table. Indeed he continued until his bleeding time had become dangerously prolonged. Early in his career he was a nutritionist of some distinction and is credited with playing a major part in determining the food ration that citizens should be allowed during and after WWII. He founded the International Nutrition Foundation in the grounds of his own home at Lady Place in Sutton Courtenay, but this never achieved the recognition he had hoped for. However the Hugh Sinclair Unit of Human Nutrition at the University of Reading, set up with an endowment from the proceeds of the sale of Sinclair's estate, has not only perpetuated his name but achieved some distinction in the field of nutrition. Sinclair himself is remembered by his DNB biographer as 'a difficult man to work under, with or over'.

Holman Hunt's 1890 painting of May Day on Magdalen Tower in the Lady Lever Art Gallery, The Wirral, has a recognizable portrait of Professor Burdon Sanderson (see arrow), the first Professor of Physiology

The University of Oxford's Botanic Garden is the oldest botanic garden in Great Britain, having its origins in a beneficent gift of £5,000 from Sir Henry Danvers in 1621 to set up a physic garden for *'the glorification of God and for the furtherance of learning'.* This mission statement is carved in Latin on the stone arch at the entrance to the Garden.

The foundation was a response to pressure from Thomas Clayton, the Regius Professor of Medicine, and Fellows of Magdalen College on whose ground the garden was built. However, the building of the gates and wall surrounding the Garden supervised by Neklaus Stone using local Headington stone, was on such a grand scale that the money ran out before any planting was undertaken.

Jacob Bobart, the first Keeper was apparently not appointed until 1642, and even then was not paid for seven years. He made a living by selling fruit grown in the Garden. One of the yew trees

that he planted is still alive. It is most appropriate that the oldest plant in a former physic garden is a yew tree as this species is now the source of the drug taxotere, which is used in the treatment of breast, ovarian and cervical cancer.

The fertility of the Garden has been attributed not only to the fact that it was established on the site of a former Jewish Cemetery, but that Bobart imported 4000 cart loads of 'muck and gunge' to raise the level of the garden which he thought was too low and in danger of flooding from the river.

The Garden is now a national reference collection of 7,000 different types of plants, making it the most compact yet diverse collection of plants in the world. There is even more biological diversity here than in tropical rain forests and other biodiversity hotspots.

Much of the boundary between the Botanic Garden and Magdalen College is occupied by the Daubeny building. Charles Daubeny was so dismayed by the dismal Chemistry laboratory and lecture room in the basement of the Old Ashmolean museum that he decided in 1848 to build a new one at his own expense. Here he was able to house his extensive geological and chemical collections and to welcome students into a modern lecture room and laboratory. The inscription above the entrance to the building, *Sine experientia nihil sufficienter sciri potest* (Without experiment nothing can be known sufficiently), is from Roger Bacon's *Opus Majus*, written in 1267-8 (see Outlier Site B).

Now immediately outside the gates of the Botanic Garden we move into the 20th century to view the Penicillin Memorial Garden in front of the Daubeny building.

The Roger Bacon inscription on the Daubeny building

The Daubeny building and the Penicillin Memorial stone

The memorial plaque to the first Jewish Cemetery outside London

The main gateway with a bust of Henry Danvers and Statues of Charles I and Charles II

Mrs Mary Lasker made her offer to endow a memorial rose garden on 18th Nov 1952. Magdalen College, who own the land on which it stands, accepted her offer on 3rd Dec 1952.

Sir John Betjeman, a graduate of the College and one of Britain's leading gurus of architectural and landscape design, got wind of the proposal and wrote to one of the senior fellows expressing his strong opposition to the idea and describing the garden as 'awful suburbanisation'. Valerie Finnis from the Waterperry Horticultural School outside Oxford was even more damning. In January 1955 she described the garden as 'a monstrous parody of an English garden'. A little later, in 1957, Hugh Sinclair, then Vice-President of Magdalen College, said that the garden was 'flourishing in all its hideousness'.

Despite these early criticisms and ongoing debates about its appropriateness to the site, we should nevertheless remember that this garden commemorates arguably the most important medical advance of the 20th Century.

The memorial stone, and those it commemorates, are shown here. (See Site 31 for more on penicillin.)

On leaving the Memorial Garden we walk west along High Street until we reach The Examination Schools (Site 4).

E.P. Abraham

E. Chain

C.M. Fletcher

H.W. Florey

M.E. Florey

A.D. Gardner

N.G. Heatley

M.A. Jennings

J. Orr-Ewing

A.G. Sanders

THIS ROSE GARDEN WAS GIVEN IN HONOUR OF THE RESEARCH WORKERS IN THIS UNIVERSITY WHO DISCOVERED THE CLINICAL IMPORTANCE OF PENICILLIN. FOR SAVING OF LIFE, RELIEF OF SUFFERING AND INSPIRATION TO FURTHER RESEARCH ALL MANKIND IS IN THEIR DEBT. THOSE WHO DID THIS WORK WERE

E.P ABRAHAM   E.CHAIN
C.M. FLETCHER   H.W. FLOREY
M.E. FLOREY   A.D. GARDNER
N.G.HEATLEY M.A JENNINGS
J. ORR-EWING   A.G.SANDERS

Presented by the
ALBERT and MARY LASKER FOUNDATION
New York · June 1953

The Examination Schools in the early evening, viewed from Merton Street

4 Examination Schools 1882

The Examination Schools were designed by Sir Thomas Jackson in the Elizabethan style of Kirby Hall in Northamptonshire. It was built on the site of the famous Angel Inn, a landmark in Oxford since 1510, and the site of Oxford's (indeed Britain's) first Coffee House opened by Jacob, a Lebanese Jew, in 1650. The new building replaced the old 'schools' which were taken over by the Bodleian Library.

The carvings over the front entrance, representing a *viva voce* examination and a degree ceremony, bring back memories to generations of students who have spent many anxious hours inside this building.

A rather different function was served by the examination schools during WW1. They became part of

'The viva voce examination' above the main entrance in High Street

the 3rd Southern Central Hospital throughout the war of 1914-18. Other wounded soldiers were housed in University and Somerville colleges, and in tents in New College gardens (see Site 6).

Now if time permits, take a diversion north up Longwall Street, bringing you to the next three sites.

In this building in 1912, William Morris built his first car, the prototype for the bullnose Morris Oxford. Thus the origins of Cowley's massive motor factories were laid here, in the shadow of New College and the old City Wall.

William Morris

The original Morris cycle works in Longwall Street

During the 1930s, Morris gave a number of generous donations to several medical causes in Oxford culminating, in 1936, with the Nuffield Medical Benefaction of £2,000,000 supporting four new clinical chairs. Hugh Cairns was elected as Nuffield Professor of Surgery on 27th January 1937, Robert Macintosh Nuffield Professor of Anaesthetics on Feb 1st, John Chassar Moir Nuffield Professor of Obstetrics and Gynaecology in May, and Leslie Witts Nuffield Professor of Medicine in November. Later a fifth Nuffield chair, that of Orthopaedic surgery, was added and Gaythorne Girdlestone was appointed as first professor.

The Regius Professor at the time, Sir Farquhar Buzzard, became a close colleague and friend of Morris (Lord Nuffield from 1938), and he should take much of the credit for encouraging Nuffield to give generously to Oxford Medicine. This was apparently not too difficult since William Morris had, as a boy, expressed a desire to study medicine but his family didn't have enough money for him to do so. How fortunate for Oxford medicine!

The main gate leading off New College Lane

When founded, the College was 'new' in several ways. Not only was it the new college dedicated to the Blessed Virgin Mary (Oriel already having been dedicated to her), but it was the first college for undergraduates, the first in which the senior members of the college had tutorial responsibility for undergraduates, and the first to be designed around the familiar quadrangle plan.

The college's origins lay in the Black Death, the plague that ravaged 14th century England. The plague was particularly hard on the clergy. It also left large parts of cities empty of their previous population. New College was intended to help to replace the missing clergy, and there was space in Oxford for a new college. That space, however, was described as *the worst plague spot*

in Oxford, where filth, rotten corpses, intestines of corpses, the dump of the refuse of the town, where thieves and malefactors lie in wait for opportunities of thieving, homicide and other intolerable evils. Not surprisingly, therefore, it is thought to have been the site of a medieval gallows. An infamous use of those gallows has recently been commemorated with the erection of a plaque to the four catholic martyrs, George Nichols, Richard Yaxley, Thomas Belson and Humphrey Pritchard, who were executed there on 5th July 1589.

Plaque to commemorate the four catholic martyrs

William of Wykeham (c. 1320-1404), the founder of New College, was Bishop of Winchester; he also served as Chancellor of England, in effect the ancestor of the prime minister. Among his achievements were the building of St George's Chapel and much of Windsor Castle, and the financing of continuous war with France. New College was his solution to the problem of finding talented young men of humble origins and good education to serve both church and state. So Wykeham had a project and a site, and in King Richard II he had a royal patron who guaranteed that the college would be built without obstruction. He is also remembered as the author of the famous motto 'manners makyth man' which appears on the garden gates.

An interesting but little-known plaque is hidden away on the southern wall of New College garden commemorating *the use of the garden as part of the Third Southern Central Hospital throughout the war of 1914-18 and to mark the spot where a way of access was made to the hospital in the schools.*

7 Holywell Cemetery

The final resting place of many of Oxford's distinguished doctors including George Rolleston 1881, Henry Acland 1900, Henry Mallam 1906, Ernest Ainley-Walker 1935 and Hugh Cairns 1952.

The land for the cemetery was given by Merton College in 1847. It has a long and interesting history. In 1086 in the Domesday book it was listed as a meadow. In medieval times a village community of fullers and weavers lived there, with a manor house, church and Holy wells – hence its current name. Holywell Green was enclosed during the Civil war.

The 'Friends of Holywell Cemetery' was formed in 1987 to maintain the cemetery as a wildlife sanctuary as well as a dignified resting place.

Contrasting tombs of the Acland family and the Ainley-Walkers

Returning to the High Street where we turn right, we will then see on the north side of the road, Site 8 – Queen's College.

Queen's College

Named after Philippa, King Edward III's wife, by her chaplain Robert de Eglesfield who founded the College in 1341. (cf Queens' College, Cambridge – founded by two Queens of England – first in 1448 by Margaret of Anjou, wife of King Henry VI and secondly in 1465 by Elizabeth Woodville, wife of King Edward IV). Queen Phillipa was said to be the foremost patron of physicians in 14th century England.

Sir John Floyer was an engaging Queen's graduate from the golden years of the mid 17th century and a contemporary of John Radcliffe at 'Univ' across the High. He matriculated, aged 15, in 1664, and remained in Oxford until 1676, when he returned to Lichfield, his home town. He wrote extensively on asthma, the pulse, and the benefits of cold bathing. He left his valuable medical library to the College on his death. That, together with the more extensive collection left a few years later by Dr Theophilus Metcalfe, resulted in Queen's

College having one of the best collections of medieval medical texts in the university. Michael Johnson and his son, who became the famous lexicographer Dr Samuel Johnson, were patients and friends of Floyer's in Lichfield.

In 1963 Lord Florey (see Site 31) was appointed as Provost of Queen's College and thus became the first male doctor of modern times to be elected to the headship of an Oxford College. Several others have since followed him (and it should perhaps be noted that Dame Janet Vaughan had preceded him by her appointment as Principal of Somerville in 1945 (see Outlier Site E). Sir Edward Abraham, of penicillin and cephalosporin fame, was an undergraduate and subsequently Honorary Fellow at Queen's. In 1966, the college named their new, architecturally controversial, James Stirling designed student hostel, over Magdalen bridge off St Clements, the 'Florey Building'.

University College owes its origins to William of Durham, who died in 1249. A legend grew up in the 1380s that it was really founded even earlier, by King Alfred in 872, and, understandably enough, this became widely accepted as the truth. Nowadays, however, William of Durham is acknowledged to have been Univ's true founder, but that still gives it a claim to be the oldest College in Oxford or Cambridge.

As Univ slowly grew in size and wealth, work began in 1634 to replace its medieval buildings with a new Front Quad, paid for by gifts from many Old Members. Although half the new Quad was finished by 1640, it took almost thirty years to complete the remainder, because of the Civil War. The College was luckier with its other main quadrangle, Radcliffe Quad, built in only three years, 1716-1719, thanks to a bequest from one Old Member, John Radcliffe, whose statue can be seen there (see page 16).

In the eighteenth century, Univ became one of the most intellectually active Colleges in Oxford: former students and Fellows could be found in senior positions in the government and the judiciary. One of Univ's early scientists was Edmund Cartwright, the inventor of the power

University College

loom. The early nineteenth century, however, was a less distinguished period: the poet Percy Bysshe Shelley came here in 1810, but was expelled the following year for publishing an anti-Christianity book *The Necessity of Atheism.*

Dr John Radcliffe (1652-1714)

One of Oxford's major benefactors, John Radcliffe, bequeathed £140,000 for the enlargement of University College, the endowment of travelling medical scholarships, and the building of a library. Any residue, his trustees were to apply 'to such charitable purposes as they in their discretion should think best'. His testamentary wishes were gradually implemented during the eighteenth and nineteenth centuries, and the Radcliffe Trust still flourishes today.

Notable twentieth-century Univ graduates

Two Prime Ministers have been associated with Univ: **Clement Attlee** was an undergraduate, **Harold Wilson** a Fellow.

Other political leaders include: **President Bill Clinton**, and **Bob Hawke**, Prime Minister of Australia.

Outside politics, recent Old Members of Univ include: **William Beveridge**, social reformer and author of the Beveridge Report; **Professor Stephen Hawking**, physicist; **C. S. Lewis,** author of the Narnia books; **Andrew Motion**, Poet Laureate; **V. S. Naipaul,** novelist and Nobel Prize-winner; **Michael York** and **Warren Mitchell,** actors; **Paul Gambaccini,** broadcaster, and – perhaps the most exotic of them all – **Prince Felix Yusupov,** assassin of Rasputin.

Radcliffe was born in Wakefield in 1652 into a middle class family; his father was an attorney and governor of Wakefield prison. He attended Wakefield grammar school and matriculated in Oxford on March 23rd 1666 aged only thirteen. On graduating from University College, Radcliffe became a Fellow of Lincoln College in 1670. He studied and then practised medicine in Oxford where he was dismissive of Hippocratic and Galenic scholarship and took Willis and Sydenham as his role models. He refused to take 'holy orders' and so had to leave his fellowship at Lincoln. He moved to London in about 1677 where he proved himself to be one of the most successful physicians of his time. His skill at diagnosis soon established his reputation among the moneyed classes and brought him to the notice of the royal family. He thus amassed a considerable fortune.

The Radcliffe trustees applied the residue of the estate to other major enterprises in Oxford: The Radcliffe Library (Camera from 1869) was built

Portrait of John Radcliffe by Sir Geoffrey Kneller (1712)

in 1737-49 to the design of James Gibbs. The Radcliffe Infirmary opened in 1770, the Radcliffe Science Library in 1902, and the John Radcliffe Hospital in 1970.

The Statue in Radcliffe Quad at Univ by Francis Bird (1667-1731) shows John Radcliffe holding the staff of Aesculapius, God of Medicine.

En intra sua moena votiva radclivium qui collegium hoc divino ingenio alumnus olim ornavit benevolentia dein quoad vixit summa fovit munificentia pari morlins amplificavlt
(Here within the walls he built stands Radcliffe in the college which he as a pupil adorned by his high talent, which through all his life he helped with unbounded kindness, and which at his death he so munificently enlarged.)

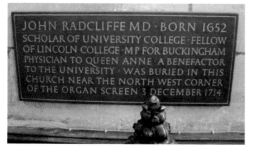

JOHN RADCLIFFE MD · BORN 1652
SCHOLAR OF UNIVERSITY COLLEGE · FELLOW
OF LINCOLN COLLEGE · MP FOR BUCKINGHAM
PHYSICIAN TO QUEEN ANNE · A BENEFACTOR
TO THE UNIVERSITY · WAS BURIED IN THIS
CHURCH NEAR THE NORTH WEST CORNER
OF THE ORGAN SCREEN 3 DECEMBER 1714

John Radcliffe was buried in the University Church of St Mary the Virgin. In spite of an impressive funeral service, no monument was erected there, as had been originally intended, and his grave was rediscovered only by chance in 1819. As recently as 1953, a memorial tablet (see left) was placed in the church on the north wall of the nave.

This painting by J.M.W. Turner 'High Street, Oxford' on loan to the Ashmolean Museum from the Loyd Collection (Copyright: Ashmolean Museum, Oxford), shows University College on the left, the Warden's house of All Souls College on the right, and Carfax in the distance. Town is represented on the left by workmen pulling down Deep Hall and boys gathering up spilled oranges, and Gown is on the right

Logic Lane (left) **leads off the High Street next to University College. It was known as Horseman (or Horsemull) Lane in the 13th and 14th centuries since there was a horse-mill here.** By the seventeenth century it had acquired the name of Logic Lane, after the school of logicians at its north end. There is a gate at each end of the lane, which is locked at night: a notice states that it is open from 7am to 8.30pm in winter, and 7am to 11pm in summer. It has one of the oldest surviving street names in Oxford. William Tuckwell in his *Reminiscences of Oxford* says: 'Only Logic Lane, quoted in The Spectator as commemorating medieval combats, not always of words alone, between Nominalists and Realists, no-one was profane enough to change'.

On the wall of University College in High Street, opposite All Souls College is a prominent stone tablet much photographed by tourists but generally ignored by residents. The inscription reads:

In a house on this site between 1655 and 1668 lived Robert Boyle. Here he discovered Boyle's Law and made experiments with an air pump designed by his assistant Robert Hooke, inventor, scientist and architect, who made a microscope and thereby first identified the living cell.

Both men were among the first members of the Royal Society, of which Hooke became Secretary in 1677.

Stone tablet to Robert Boyle and Robert Hooke

Robert Boyle (1627-1691) the seventh son of the First Earl of Cork ('The Great Earl'), settled in Oxford in 1654. Although he had no formal position in the university, he attracted several university men to join his 'circle' and he employed Robert Hooke as his assistant. Their experiments on air and vacuum led, in 1662, to the formulation of Boyle's Law which states that the pressure and volume of a gas are inversely proportional.

The portrait above of Boyle is in the basement of the Museum of the History of Science in Broad Street.

Robert Boyle

After leaving Oxford, Hooke became Gresham Professor of Geometry at Gresham College, London, where he had a set of rooms and where he lived for the rest of his life. He also served the Royal Society as secretary and publisher of the Philosophical Collections in the late 1670s and early 1680s.

Robert Hooke (1635-1703), who had been educated at Christ Church, is perhaps best known for his invention of the compound microscope and the air-pump used for experiments with Boyle, and for his book *Micrographia,* published in 1665. But he has also been credited with the invention of the quadrant, and of the Gregorian telescope. A law of elasticity has been named after him. There are replicas of his compound microscope and of his air-pump in the Museum of the History of Science in Oxford.

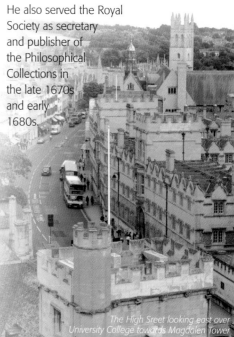

The High Sreet looking east over University College towards Magdalen Tower

Merton College was founded in 1264 by Walter de Merton, Chancellor of England and Bishop of Rochester.

Walter's conception of a self-governing community of scholars, with its own statutes and endowment, residing in buildings laid out in staircases and quadrangles, created a model for Oxford and Cambridge colleges founded in the succeeding centuries. Merton is one of three ancient Oxford colleges founded in the thirteenth century. The College buildings, set in extensive gardens and grounds, are of exceptional historical and aesthetic interest. The Library is probably the oldest surviving working library in the United Kingdom, and the Hall, Chapel, Lodge and Mob Quadrangle also date from the College's early years. The Gatehouse dates from the early fifteenth century, when Henry V granted a royal 'license to crenellate', which allowed for the construction of the battlement tower above the present-day Lodge.

Notable members of Merton College include:

John of Gaddesden (1294)
Archbishop Thomas Bradwardine (c.1321)
John Wyclif (1356)
Sir Thomas Bodley (1563)
Sir Henry Savile (1565)
Admiral Robert Blake (1615)
Dr William Harvey (1645)
Sir Richard Steele (1691)
Cardinal Newman (1825)
Lord Randolph Churchill (1867)
Sir Max Beerbohm (1890)
Professor Frederick Soddy* (1895)
F E Smith (1896)
Sir Basil Blackwell (1907)
T S Eliot (1914)
Andrew (Sandy) Irvine (1921)
Lennox Berkeley (1922)
Louis MacNeice (1926)
Edmund Blunden (1931)
Leonard Cheshire (1936)
Professor J R R Tolkien (1945)
Professor Niko Tinbergen* (1949)
Sir Roger Bannister (1950)

William Harvey (1578-1657) was born in Folkestone on 1 April 1578. He went to King's School, Canterbury, studied at Gonville and Caius College, Cambridge and then at the University of Padua, Italy. He graduated doctor of arts and medicine in 1602. He then moved to London. The portrait of Harvey shown here is said to probably be an accurate likeness. In 1604, Harvey married Elizabeth Browne, daughter of a physician to Queen Elizabeth I and King James I. This meant that Harvey met a lot of rich and wealthy people and he quickly climbed the career ladder. There were only about forty fully qualified doctors

Portrait of William Harvey in Merton College

CLOSED TO THE PUBLIC

Merton College Lo

Despite having the support of Fellows of the College, Harvey lost patients after his work was published. His theory cast doubt on bloodletting (a very common practice by medical practitioners from ancient times through to the eighteenth century) and it was only after his death that others became convinced that he was right.

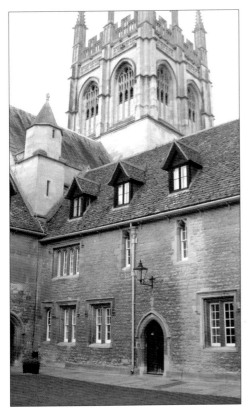

Merton tower seen from Mob quad

like Harvey in London at this time, and their fees were very high. He was selected as physician to King James I in 1618 and later to King Charles I. He was appointed physician to St Bartholomew's Hospital in 1609, although his Royal duties interrupted his work there. He followed King Charles I to Oxford and the battle of Edgehill during the Civil War, returning to London after the fall of Oxford to the parliamentary forces in 1646.

It was in 1628, 26 years after he graduated from Padua University, that Harvey published his description of the circulation of the blood in *Exercitation anatomica de motu cordis et sanguinis in animalibus* (an anatomical disputation on the movement of the heart and blood in animals). Generally known as *De Motu Cordis*.

Oxford's First Textbook of Medicine: John of Gaddesden's *Rosa Medicinae* 1314

Merton College library not only has three different printed editions of the *Rosa* – printed in Pavia in 1492 by Johannes Antonius Biretta, edited by Nicolaus Scyllatius Siculus, printed in Venice in 1502, and printed in Augsburg in 1595 (in two volumes) – but also a manuscript copy in its original 14th century binding.

14th century manuscript of John of Gaddesden's Rosa Medicinae (Merton MS 262) *2 volume edition, Augsburg, printed by Michael Manger, 1595*

Other manuscript versions of the *Rosa* are known to exist in the Bodleian, in the British Library and in Exeter Cathedral Library (an illuminated version). John of Gaddesden is widely believed to have been the model for Chaucer's 'doctor of physic'.

Title page to Pathologiae Cerebri, 1667. This engraving of Willis aged 45 and signed D Loggan delin et sculp., published in 1667, is the best likeness and only surviving portrait of Willis executed during his lifetime (Library of Christ Church, Oxford)

Plaque to Thomas Willis on the wall of Beam Hall (No 4 Merton Street)

Beam Hall, once the home of Thomas Willis, became a secret meeting place for Royalists between 1647 and 1660 (including Gilbert Sheldon), and was also the site for early meetings of the 'experimental philosophy club'.

Thomas Willis, who is considered to be one of the greatest neuroanatomists of all time, matriculated at Christ Church in 1637, took a BA in 1642, and BM in 1646. Willis studied anatomy with William Petty and was involved in the resuscitation of Anne Green in December 1650 (see Site 15). From 1644 to 1646 he served with the Royalist legion under the Earl of Dover.

He was appointed Sedleian Professor of Natural Philosophy in 1663 and published *Cerebri Anatome* in 1664. (This also involved Richard Lower, Christopher Wren and Thomas Millington). Willis introduced the word 'neurology' into medicine.

Just along Merton Street from Beam Hall is Postmasters Hall where this plaque to the memory of **Anthony à Wood,** antiquarian, is found. It is thanks to Wood's diaries that we owe so much of our knowledge of the characters of mid and late 17th century Oxford.

Beam Hall, Merton Street

Originally founded by Cardinal Wolsey as Cardinal College in 1524. The college buildings took over the site of St. Frideswide's Monastery, which was suppressed by Wolsey to fund his college.

The monastery dated back to the earliest days of Oxford as a settlement in the 9th Century. It commemorated Oxford's patron saint, Frideswide who, according to legend lived from about 665 to 735. She displayed remarkable healing powers which resulted in her shrine becoming a place of pilgrimage, and even today the present shrine in the cathedral (probably from about 1289 and restored in the late 19th century) is much visited and admired.

When Wolsey fell from power in 1529 the College became the property of King Henry VIII. He re-founded the College in 1546 and appointed the old monastery church as cathedral of the new diocese of Oxford. The new institution of cathedral and university college was named Aedes Christi, which is rendered in English as Christ Church. It is due to its ecclesiastical function that Christ Church's principal, the Dean, is always a clergyman.

During the English Civil War (1642–1646) King Charles I lived at Christ Church. (His wife, Queen Henrietta, lived in Merton College). Charles held his Parliament in the Great Hall and attended services in the Cathedral. After the war and the restoration of the monarchy in 1660, the College was rewarded for its loyalty to the House of Stuart by raising enough money to complete the main quadrangle (Tom Quad). A former student, Sir Christopher Wren, was commissioned to design a new bell tower in 1682, which houses the bell, Great Tom, from which the tower and the quad get their names. The Dean who supervised this work, John Fell, was an unpopular man who inspired the famous verse, *'I do not love thee Doctor Fell, why I don't I cannot tell, but this I know and know full well, I do not love thee Doctor Fell.'*

Famous Students

(NB Christ Church Fellows are known as 'Students')

Christ Church, known also as The House, has had many undergraduates who have subsequently gone on to achieve considerable fame. Among these are:

Physicians: **Richard Lower** and **Thomas Willis**

Scientist: **Robert Hooke**

Philosopher (and medic): **John Locke**

Religious leaders: **John Wesley** and **William Penn**

Writers: **W.H. Auden** and **Lewis Carroll**

Albert Einstein studied at Christ Church briefly in the 1930s.

The College also has a close connection with government. It has produced thirteen Prime Ministers and numerous Cabinet ministers, bishops, and civil servants. The House's most celebrated political alumnus is **William Gladstone,** who was Prime Minister four times during the 19th Century. More recently, broadcaster **David Dimbleby,** composer **Howard Goodall**, and Archbishop of Canterbury **Rowan Williams** were undergraduates at Christ Church.

Stained glass window in Christ Church Hall commemorating (from left) Willis, Acland, Garrod and Osler

Christ Church has also been the College of all Regius Professors of Medicine (RPM) since the chair was founded by King Henry VIII in 1546. He appointed John Warner, who was also Warden of All Souls College, as first Regius Professor. Many of the early RPMs were ineffective as leaders of Oxford medicine, but in the second half of the 19th centruy Sir Henry Acland initiated many changes, notable amongst which were: improvements to public health via a clean water supply and sewage disposal, introduction of the Honours School of Natural Science, and the building of the Natural History Museum, in which his lifelong friend John Ruskin was also much involved (see Site 25).

The current RPM, the 30th in direct line, is Sir John Bell, formerly a Rhodes scholar and like his famous predecessor, Sir William Osler, a Canadian. Since WWII, the RPMs have been Sir George Pickering, Sir Richard Doll, Sir Henry Harris, and Sir David Weatherall. They have all left their distinctive mark on the medical school and it will be interesting to see how history remembers them, and if any of them will displace Osler from his position as 'most famous Regius'.

Osler's successor, Sir Archibald Garrod, is thought by many of today's leading scientists to have been grossly undervalued by his contemporaries. His discovery of 'inborn errors of metabolism', and his realization that they were single gene disorders, is now seen as a giant step forward in the understanding of the molecular mechanisms of disease.

John Ruskin and Henry Acland at their last meeting in 1893 at Brantwood, Ruskin's home

In April 1324, Adam de Brome, an official in the Royal Chancery, obtained a licence to endow a small body of scholars to be called the 'House of Blessed Mary'. It is not clear whether this body ever actually existed; within two years Adam persuaded King Edward II to refound the college, which the king did in January 1326. Later that year, with the king facing the rebellion which led to his overthrow, the College prudently sought a new patron in the Bishop of Lincoln. In 1329, King Edward III gave the Hospital of St Bartholomew to Oriel. It had been founded in about 1100 as a leper hospital and served the College as a plague house. (See Outlier Site A)

Oriel never had the large estates of some of the richer colleges, but there was one important possession: Oriel was, and is, the Rector of St. Mary the Virgin, the University church used for official functions. Quite apart from the valuable consideration of the Rector's property and tithes, this gave the College a constitutional importance in Oxford.

There are no particularly famous medics amongst Oriel's alumni, but the Nuffield Professor of Obstetrics and Gynaecology is always a Fellow of the College. Moreover, Cecil Rhodes was responsible for bringing a large number of overseas scholars to Oxford who subsequently made great contributions to progress in medicine. John Keble, John Henry Newman, both key figures in the Anglican Oxford Movement, Sir Walter Raleigh (c.1552–1618), and A.J.P.Taylor are amongst the best remembered alumni.

Cecil John Rhodes (1853–1902)

(Although Rhodes was not himself involved in Medicine, the Rhodes Trust has been responsible for supporting many distinguished doctors and medical scientists, hence his inclusion here.)

Rhodes was the son of the vicar of Bishop's Stortford. He was sent as a young man to South Africa where, it was thought, the climate would benefit his weak health. It was not long before he had made a vast fortune at the Kimberley diamond diggings. At the age of twenty-eight, he returned to England in 1881 and entered Oriel College, Oxford, as a student. He eventually took his degree, and in 1899 Oxford gave him an honorary degree of Doctor of Common Law. He did not forget the University or his old college in spite of his subsequent preoccupation with the development of Southern and Central Africa.

Rhodes's benefaction to Oriel College resulted in the Rhodes Building fronting the High Street opposite St Mary the Virgin Church, completed in 1911. Designed by Basil Champneys, the building is festooned with statues of King Edward VII and King George V and sundry provosts and benefactors of the College (mainly bishops), all surmounted by the figure of Rhodes himself. The Latin inscription records that the building was erected as the result of his munificence.

Nearby, at 6 King Edward Street, there is a large metal plaque (see page 25) on the wall of the first floor, with a portrait bust of Rhodes, beneath which is the inscription:

In this house, the Rt Hon Cecil John Rhodes kept academical residence in the year 1881. This memorial is erected by Alfred Mosely in recognition of the great services rendered by Cecil Rhodes to his country.

The main monument in Oxford is Rhodes House in South Parks Road, built in 1929 as the headquarters of the Rhodes Trust, which administers the Rhodes Scholarships and other benefactions left by Rhodes to the University. Rhodes House yields a particularly rich crop of inscriptions. (See Site 27)

15 Brasenose College 1509

Brasenose College was founded by Sir Richard Sutton, a lawyer, and William Smyth, Bishop of Lincoln.

Before its foundation, part of the site was occupied by Brasenose Hall, one of the medieval Oxford institutions which began as lodging houses and gradually became more formal places of learning. The transformation of Brasenose Hall into Brasenose College was so smooth that it is difficult to give an exact date to the change. A quarry in Headington was leased to provide stone for the new buildings on 19 June 1509 and this is the year which Brasenose keeps as its foundation.

The Royal Charter, which established the body of Principal and Fellows, is dated 15 January 1511. It established a College to be called 'The King's Hall and College of Brasenose' (in this sense Brasenose Hall still exists).

William Petty 1623–1687, scientist, political economist, doctor. Brasenose's most famous 'medic' (and one of the university's most impressive polymaths).

By the time Petty was elected a Fellow of Brasenose in 1648, he had already served as a cabin boy in the Navy, had studied medicine, mathematics and chemistry on the continent, had been appointed Professor of Music at Gresham College and was taking over the teaching of anatomy in Oxford University. Within months of his election as Fellow he was granted a leave of absence and became physician to the army in Ireland, subsequently taking over the surveying of the country as well. His leaves of absence continued until 1659, when the College declared his fellowship void because of absence and his increased private income.

Petty was a founder member of the Royal Society, an inventor, statistician naval architect, cartographer and political economist, his most famous work in the latter field being his *Treatise of Taxes and Contributions* (1662).

But his popular fame rests on an event which took place when he was reader in anatomy at Oxford in 1650. The custom was for Oxford medical students to practice human dissection on the bodies of executed criminals, and Petty duly received the body of Anne Green, hanged for the murder of her illegitimate child. However, she was found to be alive, and Petty and his colleagues including Thomas Willis revived her. She went on to marry, bear three children, and live for another fifteen years.

16 St Mary's Church and Catte Street

There has been a church on this site since at least the 11th century. The oldest part of the present church is the north tower, dating from about 1280. The spire was added in 1310–20, and the Congregation House and Library (bottom left) built for the University and paid for by Thomas Cobham, Bishop of Worcester, began in 1320.

The church was the centre of university activities, including disputations, degree ceremonies, trials, etc. and the area around Catte Street was the medieval medical centre of Oxford. Convenient in the earliest days for St John's Hospital and the apothecaries shops in the High.

This street was recorded as Kattestreete in the early thirteenth century, as Mousecatcher's

Lane in 1442, and as Cat Street in the eighteenth century. In the mid-nineteenth century it was given the more respectable name of Catherine Street, but in 1930 a more robust city council restored its original name, Catte Street, together with its fifteenth-century spelling.

Dr Nicholas Tingewick lived and taught on the site that is now the All Souls Codrington Library.

The Congregation House in Catte Street was the centre of the medieval university

17 All Souls College 1438

All Souls College viewed from St Mary's Church spire

Founded by Archbishop Henry Chichele in 1438, All Souls College was dedicated to the souls of the faithful departed, particularly those who had fallen in the hundred years' war. It was said by the Archbishop to be the greatest of all war memorials.

The College always had strong medical associations; the Warden from 1536–1560 was John Warner, who was also the first Regius Professor of Medicine. In the 17th and 18th centuries the proliferation of 'physic places', which relieved the holder from taking holy orders, became a scandal as such places were usually held by non-resident members of parliament.

Its early fellowship included two of Britain's most famous physicians, namely Thomas Linacre and Thomas Sydenham.

Thomas Linacre 1460–1524 was born in Canterbury. He entered All Souls College, Oxford in 1480, and distinguished himself in Greek. He then studied in Rome,

Portrait (copy) of Thomas Linacre by William Miller 1810

gaining a knowledge of Greek and Latin, which made him one of the foremost humanistic scholars of his time. He also studied medicine at Vicenza, receiving his medical degree at Padua. Ten years later, back in England, Linacre became physician to King Henry VIII and regular medical attendant to many of the most prominent people in the country. He was also a close friend of Sir Thomas More and Erasmus. After 11 years as a physician, Thomas Linacre resigned to become a priest. He devoted the fortune from his medical practice to the foundation of chairs in Greek medicine at Oxford and Cambridge University and to the establishment of the Royal College of Physicians (1518). After Linacre obtained his charter for the College, no-one other than regular physicians could practice in and around London.

Thomas Sydenham 1624–1689 has been called the English Hippocrates, and the father of English medicine. He revived the Hippocratic methods of observations and experience. He was one of the principal

Portrait of Thomas Sydenham by Mary Beale 1689

founders of epidemiology, and his clinical reputation rests upon his first-hand accounts of gout, malarial fever, scarlatina, measles, dysentery, hysteria, and numerous other diseases. He introduced Cinchona bark into England, and praised opium.

Like his great predecessor, Sydenham emphasised accurate observations of the clinical picture. To him the foundation of medicine was not scientific examinations of anatomical and physiological conditions, but bedside experiences. He advocated no particular dogmatic system, but always tried to found his teaching on an independent reasoning. He began his exacting studies of epidemics in London in the middle of the 1650s. This work formed the basis of his book on fevers (1666), which was dedicated to his friend, the Irish-born chemist and natural philosopher Robert Boyle (1627–1691). It was later expanded into *Observationes Medicae* (1676), a standard textbook for two centuries. Sydenham also presented the theory of an epidemic constitution, i.e. conditions in the environment (air, season, etc.) which cause the occurrence of acute diseases. His treatise on gout (1683) is considered to be his masterpiece.

In the 20th century, All Souls rarely appointed scientists or doctors to its fellowship, but a notable exception was **Gwyn Macfarlane** (pictured here) who was appointed in 1963. He discovered and described the essential steps in the blood coagulation cascade. As a result he was appointed Director of the first MRC Clinical Unit for treating haemophiliacs in 1959. He was also the author of highly acclaimed biographies of both Alexander Fleming and Howard Florey (see also under Churchill Hospital, Outlier Site J1).

The Radcliffe Camera

The Radcliffe Camera with Brasenose College on the left and All Souls College on the right

The Radcliffe Camera was designed by James Gibbs and built between 1737 and 1749 with money bequeathed by John Radcliffe (1650-1714).

In his Will, Radcliffe had set aside £40,000 to acquire the land and erect a building designed to house a medical library. Guest's history of the Radcliffe Trust gives two figures for the actual expenditure: £43,226 6s 3d (£9,336.0.0. to acquire the site – many old houses had to be purchased and demolished) and £42,284 4s 10½d.

In 1860, the Trustees of Dr Radcliffe's Will transferred all books on natural sciences to premises in the University Museum, where they formed the nucleus of what is now the Radcliffe Science Library. The Camera itself was first loaned to the Bodleian Curators and later, in 1927, the Trustees presented the freehold to the University.

(NB a 'Camera' is a vaulted chamber)

This illustration shows a detail from Loggan's 1675 map of Oxford drawn before Radcliffe's library was built. St Mary's church is at the top of the map, and The Schools Quadrangle is at the bottom. The central area shows the many houses that were demolished to make way for the library

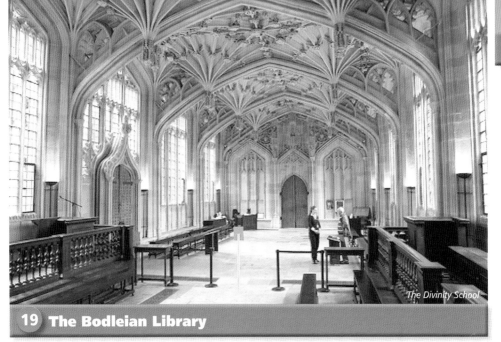

The Divinity School

19 The Bodleian Library

The oldest part of 'Bodley', the Divinity School, with Duke Humfrey Library above, was first planned in 1424 but not completed until 1490. The Divinity School has been described as 'the most beautiful room in Europe – a perfect example of 15th century perpendicular gothic.' Unfortunately, the Library was not adequately funded and was neglected. By the mid-16th century King Edward VI's commissioners had emptied it of its books and shelves!

Duke Humfrey library

Fortunately, in 1598, Thomas Bodley was so incensed that he determined to restore it. He devoted most of the remainder of his life and fortune to the task, and his Library has never looked back.

The rest of the Schools quadrangle was built 1610-1624 and 1634-1637. Of medical interest is the fact that a room on the south-west corner of the first floor was used as an anatomy teaching room. Richard Tomlin had endowed a Readership in Anatomy early in the 17th century, and teaching at this time (including the dissection of corpses of hanged criminals) was vigorous.

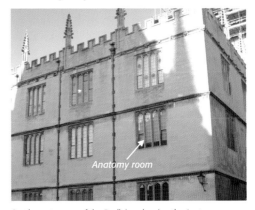

Anatomy room

South-west corner of the Bodleian showing the Anatomy room

The Sheldonian Theatre

20 The Sheldonian Theatre 1669 & Clarendon Building 1713

The Sheldonian Theatre was erected in 1664-8 to a design by Sir Christopher Wren (1632-1723) from funds donated by Gilbert Sheldon (1598-1677) who, during his long career, held office as Warden of All Souls, Bishop of London, Archbishop of Canterbury and Chancellor of the University of Oxford.

The total cost of building was £14,470 11s 11d.

Wren was at various times, an undergraduate at Wadham, a Fellow at All Souls, a collaborator of Willis in the work leading up to the publication of *Cerebri Anatome*, Professor of Astronomy at Oxford, and a member of the 'experimental philosophy club' which became the Royal Society. He also designed Tom Tower at Christ Church and St Paul's Cathedral. A true polymath indeed.

The Clarendon Building was designed by Nicholas Hawksmoor and completed in 1713 for the

The Clarendon Building

University Press, which remained there until 1829 when it moved to its present site in Walton Street. It is said to have been partly paid for by the profits from the publication in 1702-4 of Clarendon's *History of the Great Rebellion*.

East doorway of the The Old Ashmolean Museum

The museum opened on 21 May 1683. It is the oldest public museum in Britain, and the first purpose-built public museum in the world. It was built to house the collection presented to the University by Elias Ashmole (1617-92).

Much of the collection had been gathered by John Tradescant who died in 1638. The contents were universal in scope, with man-made and natural specimens from every corner of the known world. The use of the term 'Museum' was a novelty in English: it was defined as 'a study, or library; also a college, or publick place for the resort of learned men'. The Museum was designed as an integrated, three-part institution, comprising the collection itself, a chemistry laboratory for experimentation and teaching, and rooms for undergraduate lectures. Its first curator was Dr Robert Plot. It is notable that from the time of its opening, the public was admitted, a liberal measure that was by no means universally welcomed.

Old Ashmolean Museum (now Museum of the History of Science)

The Old Ashmolean has been described as 'a perfect piece of English Renaissance work' and the East doorway as 'incomparably beautiful'.

Among the many remarkable collections within are to be found some mementoes of the early work on penicillin from Florey's team at the 'Dunn School'.

22 Balliol College c.1263

John Balliol, one of King Henry III's most loyal Lords during the Barons' War of 1258-1265, was married to a Scottish Princess, Dervorguilla of Galloway. He was a wealthy man with extensive estates in England and France; his family had its roots in, and took its name from, Bailleul-en-Vimeu in Picardy. About 1260, with guidance from the Bishop of Durham, he rented a house

Original College seal

in the suburbs of Oxford, to accommodate some poor students. The foundation date of the College which grew from this is traditionally reckoned as 1263. There is actually no evidence for such precision, but we do know

that the little society John Balliol initiated was in existence by June 1266, when its dependence on him is mentioned in a royal writ. When John Balliol died in 1269, his widow Dervorguilla put his arrangements on a permanent basis, and she is honoured as co-Founder with him. She provided a capital endowment, formulated Statutes (1282), and gave the College its first seal, which it still retains.

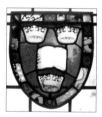

Balliol College library, built in the early 15th century, has the oldest extant representation of the university arms in one of its stained glass windows (dated 1412-17).

Nicholas Tingewick c.1300

John Wycliffe 1360s

Matthew Baillie (1761-1823)

> Nephew and pupil of **William Hunter**, Physician to King George III, author of classic text on Morbid Anatomy (1793) and Atlas (1799)

More recently:

Hugh Cairns (1896-1952), surgeon

Cyril Hinshelwood, Nobel Prize in Chemistry 1956

Baruch Blumberg (Master 1989-1994), Nobel Prize in Medicine 1976

Oliver Smithies, Nobel Prize in Medicine 2007

Sir Henry Acland (left) and Benjamin Jowett (centre) outside Balliol College c. 1890. (Photograph by Henry Taunt)

In 1869 Benjamin Jowett wrote the following to Florence Nightingale:

Dr Acland is called 'Barnum' at Oxford. He is one of the vainest, rudest men that ever lived. He is also one of the greatest bores that ever lived. But against his boring must be set that he has got one or two good things done; and against his rudeness that he is extremely kind to some persons. I believe him to be neither a man of science nor a good practitioner. He is an intolerable ass and an unendurable bore, yet a worthy man after a fashion.

(Letter of 25th July 1869)

Portrait of Matthew Baillie by William Owen RA 1823

The plaque on the wall of Balliol College commemorating 'The burning at the stake' of Latimer, Cranmer and Ridley

The New Bodleian Library

Thirteen houses were demolished to make way for the Library, including those where Sir Henry Acland lived from 1847 until his death in 1900.

Old photo showing some of the houses which were demolished. (Photograph by Sue Chaundy)

Junction of Broad Street and South Parks Road where thirteen houses were demolished in 1936 to make way for the New Bodleian Library. (Photograph by Henry Taunt)

The New Bodleian Library, built in the 1930s, was said by Jan Morris to 'look like well-equipped municipal swimming baths'. Nevertheless it is now a Grade II listed building.

The diagram (on the right) is from the 1900 Ordnance Survey map in Miriam Freeborn's book *The Demolished Houses of Broad Street*. The thirteen houses demolished in the 1930s to make way for the New Bodleian Library include that (originally three) occupied by Sir Henry Acland from 1847 until his death in 1900. His household included up to eight children and nine servants.

Acland's House

Founded by Nicholas and Dorothy Wadham in the reign of King James I. Nicholas Wadham, a member of an ancient Somerset family, died in 1609 leaving his fortune to endow a college at Oxford.

The hard work of translating intentions into reality fell on his widow, Dorothy. She fought all the claims of Nicholas's relations, lobbied at court, negotiated the purchase of a site and drew up the college statutes. She apparently instructed that the college library should be built above the kitchen so that the books should be warm and dry! She appointed the first Warden, Fellows and Scholars, as well as the college cook, to such effect that the college was ready for opening within four years of Nicholas's death. She added considerably to the endowment from her own resources, and kept tight control of its affairs until her death in 1618. It is amazing to realize that she never actually visited Oxford from her home in Devon to see the results of her generosity and business acumen!

Notable members of the college in its early years include Robert Blake, Cromwell's admiral and founder of British sea-power in the Mediterranean, and Christopher Wren. Wren attended the meetings of scientifically-inclined scholars, which were held in the college in the 1650s by Warden John Wilkins (Cromwell's brother-in-law) in his room above the main entrance to the college (pictured). Those attending formed the nucleus of the Royal Society at its foundation in 1660.

In the following century, the Rev Edward Stone discovered the active ingredient in willow bark. He went up to Wadham College in 1720 and later became a Fellow. From 1738 he held various livings around Buckinghamshire and Oxfordshire. Because he suffered from various 'agues' he resorted to a natural remedy known as Peruvian Bark, brought over by the Jesuits. He experimented by gathering and drying a pound of willow bark and creating a powder which he gave to about fifty persons: it was consistently found to be

Wadham College

'a powerful astringent and very efficacious in curing agues and intermitting disorders.' He had discovered salicylic acid, the active ingredient in aspirin. In 1763, he sent a letter announcing his discovery to Lord Macclesfield, President of the Royal Society. The letter survives to this day. It was not until 1853 that a more digestible compound of acetyl chloride and sodium salicylate was developed, and later marketed by Bayer, under the name aspirin.

Arthur Onslow (1708), a great Speaker of the House of Commons, and Richard Bethell, who became Lord Chancellor as Lord Westbury in 1861, were members of the college. Two twentieth-century Lord Chancellors, F. E. Smith (Lord Birkenhead) and John Simon, were undergraduates together in the 1890s, along with the great sportsman C. B. Fry; Sir Thomas Beecham was an undergraduate in 1897, though soon abandoning Oxford for his musical career. Frederick Lindemann, Lord Cherwell, Churchill's scientific adviser during the Second World War, was a Fellow of the college. Cecil Day-Lewis, later Poet Laureate, came up in 1923, and Michael Foot M.P. in 1931. Sir Maurice Bowra, scholar and wit, was Warden between 1938 and 1970.

Wadham College

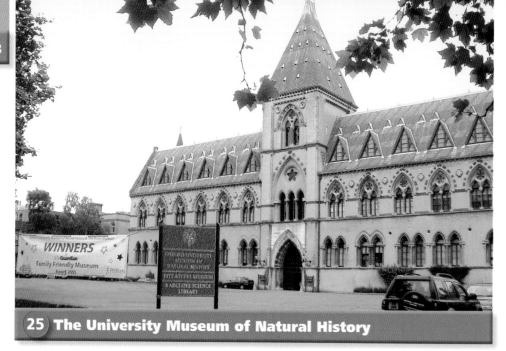

25 The University Museum of Natural History

The University Museum of Natural History houses the University's scientific collections of zoological, entomological, palaeontological and mineral specimens, accumulated in the course of the last three centuries.

The building was completed in 1860, and remains a gem of middle Victorian neo-Gothic architecture, despite suffering something of a 'credit crunch' in its later stages. Much of the planned stone carving could not be completed, as a careful examination around the door and windows will show. Up to the mid-1800s the scientific collections were scattered around the University and the Colleges, and included such important accumulations as the natural history part of the great Ashmolean Museum collections, a large comparative anatomy and physiology collection held at Christ Church, and Dean Buckland's collection of fossils.

The inspiration and drive to create a single building to house all this material, to display it, and to be the centre of the teaching of natural sciences in Oxford, came from Sir Henry Acland, the Regius Professor of Medicine. His lifelong friend, John Ruskin, was also influential in the design of the building.

This photograph (left) shows the statue of Charles Darwin in the main court of the Museum. Darwin, considered to be the father of modern biology, published the theory of evolution through natural selection in *On the Origin of Species* in 1859, only seven months before the Museum was opened.

In June 1860, the Museum was host to one of the most famous debates in scientific history. The 'great debate', held in the Radcliffe library of the museum, between Thomas Henry Huxley, 'Darwin's bulldog', and Samuel Wilberforce, then Bishop of Oxford ('soapy Sam'), concerned Darwin's theory of evolution and the questions it raised about man's unique position in the natural world, and God's role as creator.

Although there seems to be some uncertainty about the actual words used, it is generally believed that the bishop said, in a light scoffing tone, that there was nothing in the idea of evolution, and then turned to Huxley and asked was it through his grandfather or his grandmother that he claimed his descent from a monkey? At which point Huxley rose slowly and deliberately and said quietly and gravely that he was not ashamed to have a monkey as an ancestor, but that he would be ashamed to be connected with a man who used his great gifts to obscure the truth. At this point, apparently, a certain Lady Brewster fainted and had to be carried out!

Vanity Fair cartoons of Wilberforce and Huxley

26 The Radcliffe Science Library 1901

Founded under the Will of Dr John Radcliffe (1652–1714), the library was first housed in the Radcliffe Camera before being transferred to the University Museum in 1861.

In 1901, it was moved to its present location, now called the Jackson Wing, after its architect Sir Thomas Jackson (who was also responsible for the design of the Examination Schools). In 1934, an extension, the present Worthington Wing, was added after the Radcliffe Trustees had presented the Library and its holdings to the Bodleian Library. A

The Jackson Wing

further underground extension (under the lawn of the museum) which accommodates the new physical sciences reading room and a much larger bookstack, the Lankester Room, was completed in 1975.

Situated between the museum and the Library the quaintly titled 'Abbot's Kitchen' (named after the kitchen of Glastonbury Abbey) has very recently (2009) taken on a new role. It is, apparently, the new place to relax on a comfy sofa for a snack. Readers are invited to enjoy the art-deco inspired setting! The entrance is through the Library.

Abbot's Kitchen

Rhodes House

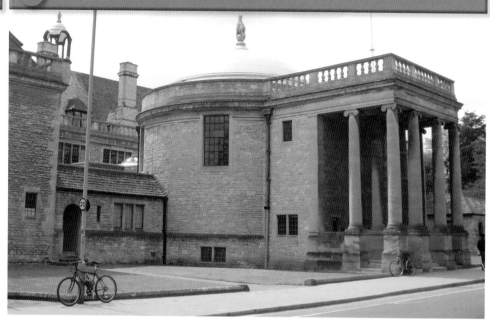

Built as a memorial to Cecil Rhodes, Rhodes House provides a headquarters for the Rhodes Trust, and facilities for educational and other purposes. It was designed by Sir Herbert Baker, architect of major public buildings in South Africa, who collaborated with Sir Edwin Lutyens on the design of New Delhi.

Rhodes Scholarships support exceptional all-round students from diverse countries: they are the oldest and arguably the most prestigious international scholarships in the world. The Rhodes Trust was established and endowed by the Will of Cecil John Rhodes, who died in 1902. Rhodes had emigrated to South Africa in 1870. He was prominent in the politics of the colony of the Cape of Good Hope (Prime Minister 1890–96). He designed his Trust to educate future leaders of the world. He had studied at Oxford and felt that its organisation especially fostered broad views and personal development.

There were originally 52 Rhodes scholarships. Currently 82 scholarships are awarded annually.

The first female scholars were selected in 1977. Cecil Rhodes directed that the selection of scholars should be based on academic ability, sporting activity, qualities of personal rectitude, strength and compassion, and sense of the public good. The Trust continues to respect the spirit of these definitions, as identified within our contemporary context. There have been over 7,000 Rhodes Scholars since the inception of the Trust. Over 4,000 are still living: these include many world leaders in politics, business, science and medicine, law, the church and academia. Cecil Rhodes should be pleased with the implementation of his vision.

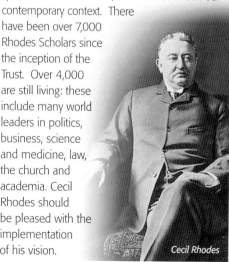

Cecil Rhodes

Dorothy Crowfoot Hodgkin (1910–1994)

Dorothy Hodgkin retains the unique distinction of being the only British female to win a Nobel Prize for science.

National Historic Chemical Landmark
The work of Dorothy Crowfoot Hodgkin
at the University of Oxford

In this building from 1956–1972 and at other times elsewhere in the Oxford Science Area, Professor Dorothy Crowfoot Hodgkin, (1910–1994) OM, FRS, Nobel Laureate, led pioneering work on the structures of antibiotics, vitamins and proteins, including penicillin, vitamin B12 and insulin, using X–ray diffraction techniques. Many methods for solving crystal structures were developed taking advantage of digital computers from the very earliest days. The work provided a basis for much of present day molecular structure driven molecular biology and medicinal chemistry.

14 May 2001

RS•C

She was awarded the Nobel Prize in Chemistry in 1964 *'for her determinations by X-ray techniques of the structures of important biochemical substances'* (including penicillin, insulin and vitamin B_{12}).

Hodgkin's work on insulin continued throughout most of the rest of her life, as indeed did her association with Somerville College. She arrived as an undergraduate in 1928, and after moving to Cambridge for her PhD was quickly attracted back to Somerville as a Research Fellow.

In her memorial service at the university church of St Mary in Oxford on 4th March 1995, Max Perutz said of her:

'There was a magic about her person. She had no enemies, not even among those whose scientific theories she demolished or whose political views she opposed … It was marvellous to have her drop in on you in the lab, like the Spring. Dorothy will be remembered as a great chemist, a saintly, tolerant and gentle lover of people and a devoted protagonist of peace.'

29 Department of Physiology

The Department of Physiology is now part of the combined Department of Physiology, Anatomy and Genetics.

Medicine has been taught at the University of Oxford for at least eight centuries, producing a succession of famous figures, and landmarks in research and learning. There was a golden period in the second half of the seventeenth century, when Harvey, Boyle, Willis, Highmore and Petty influenced physiology and anatomy profoundly, and contributed to the newly-formed Royal Society. However, Physiology as a separate Department was opened in 1883, under the direction of the first Waynflete Professor of Physiology, John Burdon Sanderson. His name is now commemorated by the newly established Cardiac Science Centre of Physiology. One of his major interests, electrophysiological research and electrophysiology, has remained a major theme of departmental research, culminating in the era of Charles Sherrington (below) and Eccles which transformed modern neurophysiology.

Sherrington won the Nobel Prize in Physiology or Medicine 1932 (shared with Edgar Adrian) 'for their discoveries regarding the functions of neurons'.

NB The Department of Human Anatomy was established as a separate entity in 1893 under Arthur Thompson, although the study of Anatomy in Oxford can be traced back to the sixteenth century. Oxford has had a succession of renowned anatomists and a notable early scientific collaboration between William Harvey and Nathaniel Highmore was on the embryonic development of the chick. More recently, in 1953 the then professor Wilfred le Gros Clark gained some fame as one of the scientists who proved that the 'piltdown man' was a hoax.

30 Department of Biochemistry 1924

Walter Fletcher, the first Secretary of the MRC, was largely responsible for persuading The Rockefeller Foundation to give £75,000 in 1924 to Oxford University to build a new Department of Biochemistry. The endowment for the first chair (Whitley) was obtained by Sherrington from a Liverpool businessman. Benjamin Moore was appointed but died soon afterwards. Rudolph Peters became effectively the first professor in 1923. Three more recent professors have won Nobel Prizes (but all largely for work done before they came to Oxford).

The Nobel Prize in Physiology or Medicine 1953 'for his discovery of the citric acid cycle'

Hans Krebs
(with Fritz Lipmann)

The Nobel Prize in Physiology or Medicine 1972 for discoveries concerning the 'chemical structure of antibodies'

Rodney Porter
(with Gerald Edelman)

The Nobel Prize in Physiology or Medicine 2001 'for their discoveries of key regulators of the cell cycle'

Paul Nurse
(with Leland Hartwell and Tim Hunt)

Dunn School of Pathology 1990

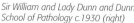

Sir William and Lady Dunn and Dunn School of Pathology c.1930 (right)

The first course of Pathology teaching was given in 1894 by John Burdon Sanderson, Professor of Physiology (Regius Professor of Medicine from 1895-1905), and Dr James Ritchie, who, in 1897, was appointed as the first University Lecturer in Pathology.

These courses were given in the Regius Professor of Medicine's Department in the Museum of Natural History. The first Department of Pathology was opened in 1901, and functioned until 1927 when it was handed over to Pharmacology on completion of the new purpose-built Sir William Dunn School of Pathology. This had been made possible by a munificent benefaction of £100,000, made in 1922 by the Trustees set up in the Will of Sir William Dunn, who died in 1912.

The Dunn School is most famous for its pioneering work on penicillin, which ushered in the antibiotic era but it also has a distinguished history in research in immunology, infectious diseases, molecular, cell and cancer biology. Its most famous staff and alumni are, not surprisingly, its Nobel prize winners pictured below.

The Nobel Prize in Physiology or Medicine 1945

'for the discovery of penicillin and its curative effect in various infectious diseases' (shared with Alexander Fleming)

Ernst Chain

Howard Florey

Dunn School Graduates with Nobel Prizes

Sir Peter Medawar *(with Sir Macfarlane Burnett)*

The Nobel Prize in Physiology or Medicine 1960 'for the discovery of acquired immunological tolerance'

Sir John Walker *(with Paul D. Boyer and Jens C. Skou)*

The Nobel Prize in Chemistry 1997 'for the elucidation of the enzymatic mechanism underlying the synthesis of adenosine triphosphate (ATP)'

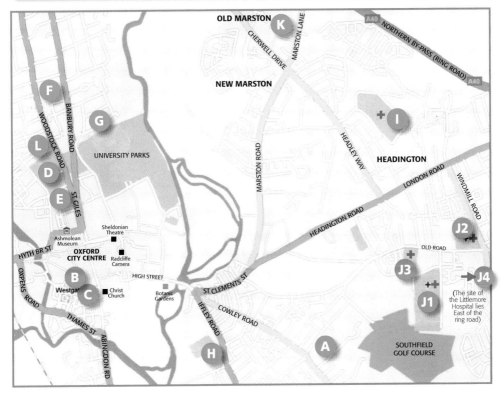

A The Hospital of St Bartholomew, *early 12th Century*

B Roger Bacon plaque c1214-1294

C Pembroke College 1624

D Radcliffe Infirmary 1770-2007

E Somerville College 1879: *Dorothy Hodgkin, Janet Vaughan*

F St Hugh's College 1886: *Hugh Cairns WWII neurosurgical hospital*

G 13 Norham Gardens: *Osler's 'Open Arms'*

H Iffley Road Athletic Track: *Roger Bannister's sub-4 minute mile*

I John Radcliffe Hospital 1972

Other Oxford hospitals

J1 Churchill Hospital

J2 Nuffield Orthopaedic Centre (Wingfield-Morris)

J3 Warneford Hospital

J4 Littlemore Hospital

K Marston Church and the Florey memorial plaque

L Green College 1979 *(Green-Templeton College from 2008), Richard Doll*

The Outlier Sites, lying beyond the parameters of the two-hour walk, are of significant historical medical interest, and I feel this guide would not be complete without them.

St Bartholomew's Chapel

A The Hospital of St. Bartholomew, Oxford

This charming reminder of our medical past is hidden at the top of a small lane on the north side of the Cowley Road between Southfield and Bartlemas roads, near Oriel College sports ground.

The Hospital of St. Bartholomew for lepers, also know as Bartlemas, was founded by King Henry I early in the 12th century (before 1129) for twelve sick persons and a chaplain, and endowed by the King with the sum of £23 0s.5d. a year, being one penny a day for each of the thirteen inmates, and five shillings a year for clothing.

In 1326, the Wardenship was granted for life to Adam de Brome, Provost of Oriel College. Two years later the King decided to make new arrangements; he granted the hospital to Oriel College, not however (as was so often the case), entirely suppressing the old foundation. The eight brethren were still to receive their 9d. a week,

and 5s. a year for clothing; there was also to be a chaplain for them apart from the Warden. However, after these expenses had been met the surplus was evidently to go to the college, and it is mentioned that the hospital would serve as a place where the sick members of Oriel might retire for a change of air.

St Bartholomew's Chapel
The small chapel was built adjoining the leper hospital, and was founded by King Henry I in 1126-1128.

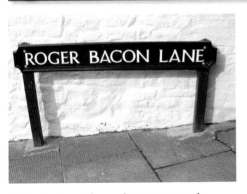

activity Near this place, in the home of his Franciscan brethren Fell asleep in Christ AD 1292.

In the court of The Museum of Natural History is a Caen stone statue of Roger Bacon (left) by Henry Hope Pinker. Bacon is depicted holding an astrolabe and callipers. The astrolabe represents his scientific studies, and the callipers suggest an aspiration to harmony (see Site 2, page 8).

Not, unfortunately, on the eponymously named Roger Bacon Lane but around the corner on the south wall of the Westgate Centre, nearly opposite the street-level entrance to the car park, and overlooking an area of litter-strewn waste land, is a plaque, deserving a more prominent display, which records the beginnings of scientific study in Oxford in the thirteenth century.

The plaque marks the site of Greyfriars Church, which stood there from about 1246 until 1538, when Franciscan houses (together with other religious houses in England) were closed down. The Franciscan order had been founded in 1209, and the first 'Grey Friars' appeared in England in 1224, so called because of the drab colour of their habit (which is now brown). The only other reminder of their presence in the St Ebbe's area is a house in Paradise Street called 'Greyfriars'. Nearly four centuries were to elapse before the Franciscans returned to Oxford: the present 'Greyfriars' in Iffley Road was built in 1921.

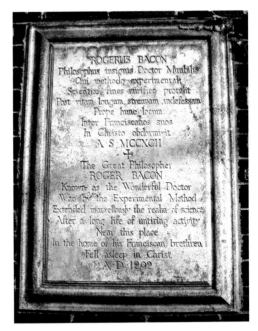

The inscription on the plaque (right) in the Westgate, records in both English and Latin, the life of one of England's most distinguished Franciscans:

The Great Philosopher, ROGER BACON, Known as the Wonderful Doctor who by the Experimental Method Extended marvellously the realm of scienc.e. After a long life of untiring

 On Aug 5th 1624, Pembroke College metamorphosed from the medieval Broadgates Hall, which had been a University hostel for law students since its construction in the fifteenth century.

The College was named after the then Chancellor of the University, William Herbert, 3rd Earl of Pembroke (whose statue stands imperiously in the Bodleian quadrangle). The endowment came from Thomas Tesdale, a merchant from nearby Abingdon, and Richard Wightwick, a clergyman from Berkshire, and enabled the conversion of Broadgates Hall into a fully-fledged college.

Dr Thomas Clayton, the last Principal of the Hall, became the first Master of Pembroke College.

He was also Regius Professor of Medicine from 1611, a post he held until 1647, when he was succeeded by his son, also named Thomas Clayton. The son, however, was not apparently of the same sound character as his father and was described as 'possest of a timorous and effeminate humour which could never endure the sight of a mangled or bloody body'. Indeed he became a figure of fun amongst his pupils.

Pembroke's place in this little guide rests on the fact that it has probably had more medically qualified heads of house than any other college. In addition to Thomas Clayton, George Pickering (also an RPM) and Roger Bannister have recently graced the office.

D The Radcliffe Infirmary 1770-2007

The first proposals to build a hospital for Oxford were made in 1758 at a meeting of the Radcliffe Trustees, who administered the estate of Dr John Radcliffe (1650-1714), physician to Queen Anne (see Site 9).

The sum of £4,000 was released for the new hospital, which was constructed on land given by Thomas Rowney, MP for Oxford 1722-1759. The honorary physicians and surgeons gave their services free, maintaining themselves by private practice, although there were junior doctors on the paid staff. The hospital depended on voluntary giving, and larger donations conferred the status

Whimsical view of John Radcliffe and Aesculapius admitting the first patients, from The University Almanack 1760

Etching of the Radcliffe Infirmary c.1835

of Governor, with the right to elect officers and recommend patients. A patient could only be admitted on a Governor's 'turn', a system which was ended officially in 1884. Some of the Governors continued to claim their right to admit patients until 1920, when a two pennies per week Contributory Scheme was introduced. Within three years this was providing 60% of the hospital's income. The first seven patients were admitted on 18th October 1770 to Lichfield (women) and Marlborough (men) wards. It is interesting to note that many sick patients were not eligible for admission, namely the mentally disordered and epileptic, those suspected of smallpox or other infectious disease, scrofula, consumption, venereal disease, chronic ulcers, inoperable cancers, pregnant women and children under seven. A list of 118 rules had been drawn up about the running of the hospital and the behaviour required of patients, even including what they were allowed to read!

Much could be (and has been) written about the distinguished history of the Radcliffe Infirmary but I should like to argue that the greatest events in its history took place (quietly and unheralded) on

27th January and 12th Febuary 1941. These were, of course, the first trials of penicillin in human subjects: the culmination of more than two years of pioneering work by Howard Florey and his team at the 'Dunn School' (see Site 31).

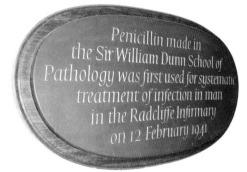

The Penicillin Plaque on the wall of the Radcliffe Infirmary

It ushered in the start of the 'antibiotic era' in medicine. The memorial plaque commemorating that event contains an interesting 'misprint'; the word systematic should really read systemic!

The final date in the RI's history that must be recorded (with a little sadness) is the date on which it finally closed its doors to patients, which was on the 14th January 2007.

Somerville was founded as Somerville Hall in 1879 to provide an opportunity for women, who until then had been excluded from membership of the University, to enter higher education in Oxford.

The founders' insistence that students should not be subjected to religious tests or obligations distinguished Somerville from its Anglican counterpart, Lady Margaret Hall, and set the ethos of cultural diversity which has characterised the College to this day. Somerville is now a mixed college for both women and men.

The choice of name for the new foundation was also significant. Mary Somerville (1780-1872), a twice-married Scot whose international reputation as a scientist was gained while raising a family of five children, provided students with a formidable role model. Her family allowed the new Hall to adopt their arms and motto (the notoriously untranslatable 'Donec rursus impleat orbem'), and over the years presented it with many family mementoes, including a number of Mary Somerville's own paintings. Its place in this guide-book rests on two outstanding medical scientists, Janet Vaughan and Dorothy Hodgkin.

Janet Vaughan, who was Principal from 1945 until 1967, had a remarkable career both as an innovative medical scientist and an outstanding administrator – impressive for someone whose headmistress had told her father that she was 'clearly too stupid to be worth educating'. In addition to her early work showing that raw liver could cure pernicious anaemia, she was prominent in developing the national blood transfusion service. At the end of WWII, Vaughan was in

Portrait of Dame Janet Vaughan by Claude Rogers

Belsen investigating how best to treat severe malnutrition, and after the war she established a reputation as one of the world's leading authorities on bone-seeking isotopes such as plutonium.

Dorothy Hodgkin (see Site 28), an undergraduate of the college from 1928 to 1931 and science tutor from 1935, was awarded the Nobel Prize in Chemistry in 1964 for her work on the structure of penicillin, vitamin B_{12}, and insulin. In addition to the numerous scientific awards and honours she received, Dorothy Hodgkin was a very popular Chancellor of Bristol University from 1970 to 1988.

Somerville College

ST HUGH'S COLLEGE BECAME THE MILITARY HOSPITAL FOR HEAD INJURIES FROM 1939 TO 1945
To commemorate
the skill and devotion of Sir Hugh Cairns FRCS and his staff,
also the patients who were treated here,
many of whom made miraculous recoveries from severe wounds.

Commemorative plaque outside the St Hugh's College library

St Hugh's was founded in 1886 by Elizabeth Wordsworth, the great niece of the poet. She had a strong sense of the historical perspective in which her new foundation would take its place.

Using money left to her by her father, a bishop of Lincoln, Elizabeth named the College after one of his twelfth century predecessors, Hugh of Avalon, who was canonised in 1220, and in whose diocese Oxford had been. Elizabeth Wordsworth was a champion of the cause of women's education, and her foundation was intended to enable poorer women to gain an Oxford education. But the college's inclusion in this guide rests on its role in WWII when Hugh Cairns, the Nuffield Professor of Surgery, turned the college into a neurosurgical hospital.

Like Florey, Cairns was born of a British father who had emigrated in the late 19th century, and an Australian mother. He qualified in Adelaide during the first world war and then won a Rhodes scholarship to Balliol College (where he soon married the Master's daughter!). After various posts in London he won a Rockefeller Scholarship and went to work with Harvey Cushing in Boston. This experience fired his interest in neurosurgery which then dominated the rest of his working life. He was appointed as the first Nuffield Professor of Surgery in 1937 having already been much involved with Lord Nuffield in plans for developing the Oxford Clinical School.

After Munich, in September 1938, Cairns formed the idea of a special hospital for head injuries at Oxford. As a planner he was supreme, and never hesitated to put his ideas forward at the highest level. Thus in a very short time the war office decided to take over St Hugh's College as a hospital for head injuries.

Cairns's work began at the hospital when it opened in February 1940. Starting with 50 beds, by the time of the invasion of Normandy, it held 430. Among the hospital's staff were the neurologists D. Denny-Brown and W. Ritchie Russell, the pathologist Dorothy Russell, and the bacteriologist G.T. ('Daddy') Western. Cairns was able to carry out research into the incidence of epilepsy after brain injury, the assessment of the psychological state of the brain-injured patient, and electroencephalography. Work was also carried out on the nature of concussion. From 1943 Cairns worked closely with Howard Florey in assessing the value of penicillin in treating and preventing wound infection. They travelled together to front line military hospitals in North Africa, where penicillin treatment was pioneered.

Early in the war Cairns designed, and had constructed, eight mobile neurosurgical units, to operate close to the action so that soldiers with head injuries could be treated quickly. He was also responsible for introducing specially designed crash helmets for army motorcyclists, thereby dramatically reducing their injuries.

Sadly, a rare lymphosarcoma of the caecum brought about his untimely death in the Radcliffe Infirmary, Oxford, at the early age of fifty-six, on 18 July 1952. His tomb is in Holywell Cemetery (see Site 7).

13 Norham Gardens was built for The Public Orator when University personages first began to live with their families outside Colleges, and is described in the most authorative architectural treatises of the time. It belonged for a while to the Conybeare family whose son John became the writer of the foremost *Textbook of Medicine* and was the outside Assessor (from London) for both the utilisation of the Radcliffe Observatory as a Laboratory and for the appointment of the first Nuffield Professors.

13 Norham Gardens in 1906

The Oslers purchased the house in 1906, whereupon it became 'The Open Arms' hosting thousands of guests, especially from America. It was visited by Mark Twain and by Rudyard Kipling. The Oslers lived there until their deaths, he in 1919 and she in 1928. The house was left to Christ Church as the residence of the Regius Professor of Medicine. Regius Professors Sir George Pickering and Sir Richard Doll made it their home, as did Lord Walton, Warden of Green College after Doll. It has housed the University's Newcomers Club and The Reuters Foundation Programme in Oxford for many years. Purchased by Green College in 2001, it now houses the newly renamed Green-Templeton College's Osler-McGovern Centre.

Here, on 6 May 1954, Roger Bannister
set a new World Mile record of
3 minutes 59.4 seconds
The first Mile ever run under 4 minutes

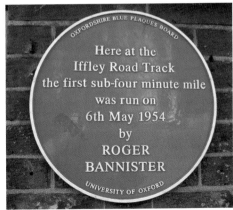

OXFORDSHIRE BLUE PLAQUES BOARD

Here at the
Iffley Road Track
the first sub-four minute mile
was run on
6th May 1954
by
ROGER
BANNISTER

UNIVERSITY OF OXFORD

The Iffley Road Athletic Track was the site of the world's first sub-4 minute mile.

Sir Roger Bannister must be one of Oxford's most famous 20th century doctors but, uniquely, his fame rests more on the fact that he was the first human being to run a mile in less than four minutes than on his work as a distinguished neurologist with a special interest in the autonomic nervous system, and College head. After first achieving this athletic feat in Oxford on

Roger Bannister setting the world record. (Photo: Oxford Mail & Times)

6th May 1954, Bannister went on to beat his arch rival, the Australian John Landy in what has been called 'the miracle mile' and 'the perfect mile' at the Empire games in Vancouver on August 7th 1954.

In 1919, the Radcliffe Infirmary purchased the Manor House estate in Headington. The Infirmary site was already overcrowded and the hospital authorities had been asked to provide sanatorium accommodation for tuberculosis sufferers. They had applied to the Radcliffe Trustees for the use of some of the Observatory land, but without success.

A public appeal for funds was launched, and much of the purchase price came from the British Red Cross as part of the winding-up of monies raised during the First World War. It was proposed that the new hospital should serve as a war memorial. Roads and drainage for a tuberculosis hospital were laid, but financial difficulties intervened. In the event, the first hospital use of the site was when the Preliminary Training School of the newly established School of Nursing took up residence in the Manor House in 1922. The Ministry of Health finally approved the plans for the hospital for tuberculosis cases, and the Osler Pavilion, named after Sir William Osler, opened in 1927.

The Infirmary's finances were still in a poor state. In May 1925, having learned that the value of the Manor House estate might be affected by a

The West Wing

proposal for an arterial road, the Governors began to sell portions of the estate for building sites. A further large portion of the site was sold in the early 1930s when the Nuffield benefactions made extensive building necessary at the Infirmary. The present site of the John Radcliffe Hospital is only about half the size of the estate purchased in 1919.

In 1960, the Manor House site was chosen for the new hospital, and a planning team was appointed in 1963. Work began on Phase I, a new maternity hospital, in 1968. This building is now the John Radcliffe Women's Centre. In the same year the Preliminary Training School left the Manor House. The maternity hospital opened in July 1972. Almost immediately the contract for Phase II was signed, and this acute hospital opened in 1979, with extensions continuing to the present day, culminating with the opening of the Children's Hospital and the West Wing in 2007.

The development of the John Radcliffe site has facilitated the rapid growth of basic and clinical research in Oxford. The openng of the Institute for Molecular Medicine in 1989 (recently renamed the Weatherall Institute to recognise its founder Sir David Weatherall) accelerated this growth. The Oxford Medical School is now recognised internationally as one of the world's leading centres of excellence for biomedical and clinical research and teaching.

The new Children's wing of the John Radcliffe Hospital

J1 The Churchill Hospital

A hospital on the Churchill site was first proposed in 1940 by the Ministry of Health with the intention that it should serve as an Emergency Medical Service hospital for local air raid casualties. This proved unnecessary, and on the completion of the buildings in January 1942 they were leased to the medical services of the United States Army. The American Hospital in Britain was invited to take over the hospital in September 1941, under the general administration of the Wingfield-Morris Orthopaedic Hospital (now the Nuffield Orthopaedic Centre). They transferred their activities from Park Prewett Hospital, Basingstoke, on 1 January 1942. The hospital was opened as the Churchill Hospital by the Duchess of Kent on 27 January 1942. When the American authorities left, Oxford City Council took over the buildings, prompted by local hospitals through the Oxford and District Joint Hospitals Board. The Committee of the Radcliffe Infirmary undertook responsibility for the hospital. Patients began to arrive in January 1946.

On 1 April 1993, the John Radcliffe Hospital and the Churchill Hospital were united as the Churchill John Radcliffe Hospital, and on 1 April 1994 the Oxford Radcliffe Hospital NHS Trust was formed, the final step in the union of the John Radcliffe and Churchill Hospitals.

The surgeons on gas mask drill, 1942

Since that time the Churchill hospital has been the site of almost continuous development. The old buildings are gradually being replaced by modern wards and research laboratories, culminating in the opening in 2009 of the massive new Cancer Centre. Despite the cutting edge research now going on in several disciplines such as oncology, genetics, epidemiology and infectious diseases, perhaps the most ground-breaking work done at the Churchill hospital was that of Professor Robert Gwyn Macfarlane CBE, FRS (1906–1987) in the 1950s and 1960s. He did much to unravel the mechanism of blood coagulation and he introduced the concept of an enzyme cascade. This work made possible the rational treatment of haemophiliacs. He has recently been described as one of the most brilliant medical scientists of his day, and the most distinguished 20th century haematologist in the UK (see Site 17, page 29).

The Wingfield Convalescent Home was opened in 1872 on the site now occupied by the Nuffield Orthopaedic Centre. It was funded by public donations, principally £1,545 from Mrs Hannah Wingfield in memory of her husband Charles, who had been a surgeon at the Radcliffe Infirmary from 1817 until his death from cholera on 10th May 1846.

In 1914 the Home became an auxiliary hospital to the Third Southern General Hospital at the outbreak of the first world war. The increase in patients led to wooden huts being built in the grounds, including orthopaedic workshops, due to the nature of many of the injuries. In 1921, the home officially became an orthopaedic hospital and in 1924 the buildings were improved and the Home became an open air hospital, with 125 beds and three private wards. A donation of some £70,000 from William Morris (later Lord Nuffield) in 1930 made the rebuilding of the hospital possible. The Prince of Wales officially opened it as the Wingfield-Morris Orthopaedic Hospital in 1933. In 1937, Gaythorne Girdlestone, who had treated patients during the first world war, became the first British Professor of Orthopaedic Surgery. He was succeeded in 1949 by Josep Trueta from Spain.

Trueta (left) was a Catalan nationalist and military surgeon exiled from Spain following the defeat of the Republicans during the Spanish civil war. He was invited to Britain to give advice and help in civil defence to the British home front in anticipation of the imminent Second World War. He worked briefly with Florey in the Sir William Dunn School of Pathology before moving as a Senior Orthopaedic Surgeon to the Radcliffe Hospital, and then in 1949 succeeding Girdlestone as Nuffield Professor of Orthopaedics, a post he held until his retirement back to Spain in 1966.

Portrait of Charles Wingfield (1786-1846)

Architect's model of the Nuffield Orthopaedic Centre

The hospital became part of the newly founded National Health Service in 1948 and was renamed as the Nuffield Orthopaedic Centre (NOC) in 1950. It became the Nuffield Orthopaedic Centre NHS Trust on 1st April 1991. Like the other Oxford hospitals, the NOC has seen huge developments in both the clinical and academic spheres.

The custom-built Botnar Research Centre, housing the Oxford University Institute of Musculoskeletal Sciences, opened in 2002.

When the Radcliffe Infirmary opened in 1770, its five-acre site off the road to Woodstock was in a rural setting well outside the city boundary. But by 1812, when there was a proposal to build a sister institution, the Radcliffe Lunatic Asylum, the area around the Infirmary was already becoming congested. So in 1813 a ten-acre site was bought in Southfield off Old Road, where land was cheaper as well as more plentiful, and the air was very much better.

The Warneford Hospital

The foundation stone of the Radcliffe (or Oxford) Lunatic Asylum was laid on 27th August 1821 by the Bishop, in the presence of the President of Trinity, the acting Pro-Vice-Chancellor, the Provost of Oriel, Sir Joseph Lock, the Proctors, Dr Williams, Dr Bourne, Dr Kidd, and other Gentlemen of the University and City. The Principal of Magdalen Hall availed himself of the opportunity to observe that such an Institution was peculiarly desirable here, as none had been erected within a day's journey of Oxford. He also remarked that it had been ascertained by parliamentary returns, that insanity was a much more common malady than was generally supposed.

The Asylum opened in 1826 'for the accommodation of lunatics selected from the higher classes of society'. It was the first of a number of hospitals to move to Headington in search of fresh air and open countryside.

Later renamed the Warneford Lunatic Asylum after the Revd Samuel W. Warneford, Rector of Bourton-on-the-Hill, Gloucestershire (who contributed the huge sum of £70,000 to it over his lifetime), the asylum aimed to recreate the atmosphere of a gentleman's country house.

An advertisement from *Kelly's Directory of Oxfordshire* in 1935, shows that the phrase 'mental patients belonging to the educated classes' had replaced the 'lunatics selected from the higher classes of society' of 88 years before.

J4 Littlemore Hospital

In the early nineteenth century, the local parish was responsible for the care of those with no means of support and this included the mentally ill, who were often accommodated in the workhouses as a result.

Under the 1808 County Asylum Act, the County Magistrates were encouraged to provide a suitable institution for the mentally ill chargeable to parishes; this was not enforced until the 1845 Lunacy Act.

In 1841, the Oxfordshire Magistrates resolved to build 'a public institution ... provided it could be done at reasonable expense'. Money was borrowed, land was purchased at Littlemore and the building was opened in 1846. Complaints that the buildings were inadequate for their purpose began very early and continued throughout the history of the hospital. The original site was finally closed in 1998, when the hospital moved to new buildings across the road.

Shortly after the opening of Littlemore, the County authorities in Oxford entered into contracts with other counties and districts for patient care. Throughout the nineteenth century, Oxford received payments from other authorities for looking after their patients at Littlemore, usually as an agreement for so many patients per year; patients came from the city of Oxford, the county of Berkshire and the boroughs of Reading, Abingdon and Windsor. As Littlemore was often overcrowded, there were also agreements from time to time for Oxfordshire patients to be cared for elsewhere, such as Bethnal Green, Buckinghamshire, Dorset, Worcestershire and Kent.

Large numbers made it inevitable that individually tailored treatment was difficult. However, although confinement, restraint, padded cells and rough treatment were all used in the nineteenth century, the staff were forbidden to strike patients (on pain of instant dismissal) and a case of mechanical restraint in 1858 was reported at length in the annual report because it was an exception. Thomas Saxty Good, Medical Superintendent 1906–1936, introduced analytical treatment methods.

In 1961, the Annual Report noted that changes in the treatment of patients had created domestic maintenance problems, as in earlier years much of this work was carried out by patients. Throughout the nineteenth century the men had helped with gardening and painting and the women had worked at needlework and in the laundry. Both sexes assisted with housework. By 1963, patients were working in the community: contracts for work were entered into with a Rural District Council for street cleansing, with the GPO for cleaning telephones, dismantling obsolete exchanges and laying pipes, and with a factory for light assembly work.

With the advent of the National Health Service, Littlemore had its own Hospital Management Committee until 1968, when it was united with the Warneford under the Isis Hospital Management Committee. Both hospitals became part of Oxfordshire Area Health Authority (Teaching) in 1974, Oxfordshire Health Authority in 1982, Oxfordshire Mental Healthcare NHS Trust in 1994, and are now part of Oxfordshire and Buckinghamshire Mental Health NHS Foundation Trust.

The building was unsuitable for modern mental health care and, when it closed in 1996, the services moved to purpose built accommodation on the opposite side of the road. The original hospital building has been preserved and the site developed as housing, under the name of St. George's Park.

The new Littlemore Hospital is a psychiatric hospital which caters for forensic psychiatry. Most of the patients have committed some form of legal offence.

The Observatory, Green College – north facade

In the village of Old Marston, which lies just inside Oxford's northern ring road, is the classic old parish church of St Nicholas, whose origins can be traced back to the 12th century. The village and church have strong associations with penicillin since three members of the team lived here. One member, Norman Heatley, lived here for over 50 years and his house has a Blue Plaque to celebrate his residence. Heatley is buried in the churchyard. In addition, in the porch of the church there is a slate plaque (left) inscribed:

In Memory of a great man a great scientist Howard Walter Florey OM FRS 1898-1968 Baron Florey of Adelaide and Marston Provost of The Queen's College Oxford. His research was devoted to uncovering the causes of disease and by his vision and leadership penicillin was placed in the hands of the physicians.

Ironically, as with the plaque in the Radcliffe Infirmary, the sculptor has had to improvise to correct two apparent spelling mistakes!

L **Green Templeton College 1979/2008**

The College was founded in 1979 around the architecturally outstanding eighteenth century Radcliffe Observatory (1773), as the result of a generous benefaction by Dr. Cecil Green. It was created to bring together graduate students in medicine and related disciplines and especially to encourage academic programmes in industry. The first Warden was Sir Richard Doll.

The Radcliffe Observatory functioned as an observatory for 160 years from 1773 until 1934, when the previous owners (the Radcliffe Trustees) decided to sell it and to erect a new Observatory in Pretoria, South Africa, where the less polluted atmosphere would be suitable for the study of the southern hemisphere. The purchaser of the Radcliffe Observatory in 1934 was Lord Nuffield, who presented it to the hospital authorities and in 1936 established the Nuffield Institute for Medical Research there. In 1979, the Institute moved to new premises in the grounds of the John Radcliffe Hospital, thus freeing the Observatory site for its new owner.

Professor Sir Richard Doll (1912–2005) was an eminent epidemiologist whose research established the causative association between smoking and lung cancer. He was appointed Regius Professor of Medicine in 1969. During his ten years in this post, he helped develop Oxford into one of the top medical schools in the world, with particular strengths in population-based studies of disease. In 1979, Doll became the first Warden of Green College, and also Director of the Cancer Epidemiology Unit.

On Doll's death, the Medical Research Council Chief Executive, Professor Colin Blakemore, said 'We have lost a great scientific mind. Professor Sir Richard Doll was one of the most important medical scientists of the 20th century. His proof of the link between smoking and cancer has done as much to save lives as the discovery of penicillin, or the development of the polio vaccine. The profound implications for health policy resonate to this day.'

Index

Index

Index